To my dear & close
friend, Ann,

May this little book
be a source of comfort
to you as our friendship
is to me.

In His Love,
Lei Lanni

Whatsoever Things

Are True

Compiled by

Harold Whaley

Library Director

for

Unity School of Christianity

Unity Books
Unity Village, Missouri
64065

Illustrations by Sue Jackson
Cover photograph by Keith McKinney

Grateful appreciation is extended to those authors who have granted permission to use their work in this compilation. Acknowledgment is also here made of the eternality of thoughts of those persons whose works exist in the public domain, for which no permission is necessary. We would also like to thank the various editors of Unity publications for granting us permission to reprint many fine poems and excerpts that originally appeared in their pages, under the copyright of Unity School of Christianity.

FIRST EDITION, April 1980.

Whatsoever Things
Are True

Because you lack a noble and successful past is no reason why you should lack a noble and successful future.

THOMAS DREIER

Everything that we are, everything that we do, everything that we say is immortal in the sense that it has its effect somewhere in the world, and that effect in turn will have its results somewhere else, and the thing goes on in infinite time and space. A man is what he thinks, and every one who has influenced him—from Socrates, Plato, and Confucius down to his parish preacher and his nursery governess—lives in him.

HU SHIH

A haze on the far horizon,
  The infinite, tender sky,
The ripe, rich tint of the cornfields,
  And the wild geese sailing high;
And all over upland and lowland
  The charm of the golden-rod,—
Some of us call it Autumn,
  And others call it God.

BLISS CARMEN

Love seeks no cause beyond itself and no fruit; it is its own fruit, its own enjoyment.

ST. BERNARD

Of all the motions and affections of the soul, love is the only one by means of which the creature, though not on equal terms, is able to treat with the Creator and to give back something resembling what has been given to it.

ST. BERNARD

Let liberty, justice, peace, love, and understanding be established in me and throughout the world, in the name of the Lord Jesus Christ.

WEEKLY UNITY

If we believe that there is a basic unity of all creation, it behooves us to emphasize that which we have in common with our fellows.

CHARLES R. FILLMORE

As long as this earth exists there will be children to bless, children to love, children who will help us grow in love, patience, and understanding, children who will bless us with happiness even as we would bless them, children who by God's blessing and ours will become strong, courageous, illumined, and helpful men and women.

CLARA PALMER

He dwells in the depths of my being, more inward than my innermost self, and higher than my highest.

ST. AUGUSTINE

Beauty is the splendor of truth.

PLATO

There is no more useful precept in one's personal self-discipline than that which bids us pay primary attention to what we do and express, and not to care too much what we feel. Action seems to follow feeling, but really action and feeling go together; and by regulating the action, which is under the more direct control of the will, we can indirectly regulate the feeling, which is not.

WILLIAM JAMES

We are children of the same God. We work in the same vineyard. The fact that we use different doors will make little difference as long as they are kept open to others.

JACOB WEINSTEIN

Be free from duplicity and stand firm in the path of truth.

PERSIAN SAYING

To forgive everybody for everything at all times, regardless of circumstances, is the first step toward complete emancipation.

CHRISTIAN DAA LARSON

If life should seem to falter,
  If friends should seem to fail,
I would not bid Thee alter
  The things 'gainst which I rail;

But cleanse, O God, my vision
  That I may clearly see,
Through senses that imprison,
  The good thou hast for me.

ERNEST C. WILSON

There is a practical way to find happiness, health, and prosperity. It is the fearless way. This way is dependent entirely upon your faith in the unfailing power of God within you. When you realize the presence of this indwelling power nothing in the world can offend or frighten you.

LOWELL FILLMORE

In the mountains of truth, you never climb in vain. Either you reach a higher point today, or you exercise your strength in order to be able to climb higher tomorrow.

NIETZSCHE

Faith is love taking the form of aspiration.
WILLIAM ELLERY CHANNING

Spiritual knowing, is of all means, the only direct means of liberation. Liberation is never accomplished without it, as sure as food is not cooked without fire.
ATMABODHA

It is within thy power, whenever thou shalt choose, to retire into thyself. For nowhere either with more quiet or more freedom from trouble does a man retire than into his own soul.
MARCUS AURELIUS ANTONINUS

Anyone can carry his burden, however hard, until nightfall. Anyone can do his work, however hard, for one day.
ROBERT LOUIS STEVENSON

We would have inward peace but will not look within.
EMPEDOCLES

After all, our worst misfortunes never happen, and most miseries lie in anticipation.
HONORÉ DE BALZAC

Today I send my heart to school.
Teach it, I pray, love's gentle rule.
Initiate me, day by day,
Into wisdom's quiet way
And bless my eyes that they may see
Life's inherent harmony,
The beauty of Thy wondrous plan,
And Christ within the heart of man.

R. H. GRENVILLE

The real fault is to have faults and not try
to mend them.

CONFUCIUS

I plant my outdoor seeds with faith
    and joy,
E'en though I do not know what secret
    power to grow they may employ;
And gladly work to do my part
To till the soil with all my heart.

I've also found a special garden in my
    soul
Where good thought seeds bear marvel-
    ous fruits that keep me whole.
I keep this hidden garden free from
    weeds
As I, with earnest zeal,
Rejoice, and use its fruits to bless and
    heal.

LOWELL FILLMORE

Rivers hardly ever run in a straight line.
Rivers are willing to take ten thousand
    meanders
And enjoy every one
And grow from every one—
When they leave a meander
They are always more
Than when they entered it.
When rivers meet an obstacle,
They do not try to run over it;
They merely go around—
But they always get to the other side.
Rivers accept things as they are,
Conform to the shape they find the
    world in—
Yet nothing changes things more than
    rivers;
Rivers move even mountains into the
    sea.
Rivers hardly ever are in a hurry—
Yet is there anything more likely
To reach the point it sets out for
Than a river?

JAMES DILLET FREEMAN

All that man can possibly do, be, or become, is now within him, an undeveloped
possibility of attainment. It is for him to
bring it forth and, in the light of a knowledge and understanding of Truth, lift it to
the plane where it belongs.

FAYETTE M. DRAKE

Our remedies oft in ourselves do lie,
which we ascribe to Heaven.

WILLIAM SHAKESPEARE

As the sun returns in the east, so let our
patience be renewed with the dawn; as the
sun lightens the world, so let our loving-
kindness make bright the house of our
habitation.

ROBERT LOUIS STEVENSON

Come ye apart and rest awhile.
   Leave the world behind;
Enter, and take refuge in
   The chamber of your mind.

In the silence, meditate
   On the Truth you know:
God without and God within,
   Around, above, below.

Trim the altar lamp of faith;
   Though its light be dim,
He is mindful of His own.
   Only turn to Him!

Quiet heart, receptive mind,
   And the Christ for guest—
He will heal and strengthen you,
   He will give you rest.

R. H. GRENVILLE

Quarrel not at all. No man resolved to make the best of himself can spare time for personal contention.

ABRAHAM LINCOLN

The great use of life is to spend it for something which outlasts it.

WILLIAM JAMES

Consider before you speak:

First: What you speak.

Second: Why you speak.

Third: To whom you speak.

Fourth: Concerning whom you speak.

Fifth: What will become of what you speak.

Sixth: What will be the benefit of what you speak.

Seventh: Who may be listening to what you speak.

Place your word on the end of your finger before you speak it;

Turn it these seven ways before you speak it;

And no harm will result when you speak it.

COUNSELS OF BARD DDOEIT

Men were born to succeed, not to fail.

HENRY DAVID THOREAU

A man wrapped up in himself makes a very small bundle.

BENJAMIN FRANKLIN

Success lies very largely in our own hands. It means effort; it means having a definite aim and striving earnestly to achieve it; it means wise planning, a knowledge of ourself, of our circumstances and possibilities; it means the power to judge truly of values.

GRENVILLE KLEISER

The task of truth-seeking is one which, to be successful, must be cooperative. When art, science, philosophy, and religion shall unite their full ministry in behalf of the accuracy, certainty, and influence of truth—becoming the willing channels of the Spirit who is to teach us all things—the day of Truth will come, and justice, goodness, and peace will reign upon the earth, filling human hearts with supernal joy.

LEETE

My good is very close to me. I take my meddling negative thoughts off my problem and let the divine law operate in my affairs.

LOWELL FILLMORE

To live content with small means, to seek elegance rather than luxury, and refinement rather than fashion; to be worthy, not respectable, and wealthy, not rich; to study hard, think quietly, talk gently, act frankly; to listen to stars and birds, to babes and sages, with open heart; to bear all cheerfully, do all bravely, await occasions, hurry never; in a word, to let the spiritual, unbidden and unconscious, grow up through the common—this is to be my symphony.

WILLIAM ELLERY CHANNING

He who is in you is greater than he who is in the world.   I JOHN 4:4

The men and women who have the divine qualities of sympathy, progress, and tolerance are forever young.

MARGARET DELAND

When you look at the world in a narrow way, how narrow it seems! When you look at it in a mean way, how mean it appears! When you look at it selfishly, how selfish it is! But when you look at it in a broad, generous, friendly spirit, what wonderful people you find in it!

HORACE RUTLEDGE

Giving thanks for our blessings is in itself a blessing. We give thanks not in order to please a vain God, but for the sake of the understanding and loving attitude it gives us. Giving thanks brings us into a greater consciousness of our oneness with God. It helps us to live up to our demonstrations after we have made them, which is just as important as making them in the first place.

JAMES E. SWEANEY

Every day that is born into the world comes like a burst of music, and rings itself all the day through; and thou shalt make of it a dance, a dirge, or a life march, as thou wilt.   CARLYLE

There is not a moment in which your character is not being shaped in one direction or another. Your life is simply the product of repeated choices. Grandeur of character is the effect of many habits. Know precisely what you want, proceed diligently toward it, and the best results will reward your diligence.

GRENVILLE KLEISER

God never closed one gap but He opened another.   IRISH PROVERB

In the rush and noise of life, as you have intervals, step home within yourselves, and be still. Wait upon God to feel His good presence; this will carry you evenly through your day's business.

WILLIAM PENN

That aim in life is highest which requires the highest and finest discipline.

HENRY DAVID THOREAU

Lord, grant me the gift of silence,
  The power to hold my peace.
When I should guard my erring thoughts,
  Prevent their blind release;

For sharp, impulsive words can wound
  Another's heart and soul,
And break the golden bond of love
  That makes mankind a whole.

Lord, set a seal upon my lips.
  Let no words, harsh or ill,
Flow from them idly. Give me, Lord,
  The grace of keeping still

Until Thy Word can speak through me
  To lift and bless and heal.
Then shall my every utterance
  Thy holy self reveal.

PRISCILLA MAY MOORE

Thoughts are things, and their airy wings
Are swifter than carrier doves.
They follow the law of the universe
And they speed o'er the track to bring you
    back
Whatever went out from your mind.
ELLA WHEELER WILCOX

As Jesus blessed and broke the bread
  To feed the hungering throng,
So we the word of Truth may spread
  Where'er we pass along.

Each loving word, each kindly deed,
  Each helping hand held forth,
The essence of His holy creed,
  Is priceless in its worth.

Unstinted may our sharing be;
  His bounty cannot fail.
His substance, blessed for you and me,
  Forever shall prevail.
BETH HINDS

The only place to find contentment and
health is in the place or state of consciousness that Christ, the Truth, has prepared
for you. These inner riches do not depend
upon outer conditions, and we must not
bind ourselves by believing that they do.
MYRTLE FILLMORE

Justice alone, fundamental as it is, will seldom kindle holiness in a soul in which the light of love is quenched, or burns but dimly. It is justice illumined with mercy that floods the world with ineffable goodness and grace.

THE TALMUD

Great works are performed not by strength but by perseverance.

SAMUEL JOHNSON

The world is my country, all mankind are my brethren, and to do good is my religion.

THOMAS PAINE

Men attract not that which they want, but that which they are.

JAMES ALLEN

Nothing in this world is so good as usefulness. It binds your fellow creatures to you, and you to them; it tends to the improvement of your own character and gives you a real importance in society, much beyond what any artificial station can bestow.

SIR BENJAMIN COLLINS BRODIE

It alters the whole outlook on life to know you personally are an idea in the mind of God.

ARCHDEACON WILBERFORCE

O believe, as thou livest, that every sound that is spoken over the round world, which thou oughtest to hear, will vibrate on thine ear. Every proverb, every book, every by-word that belongs to thee for aid or comfort, shall surely come through open or winding passages.

RALPH WALDO EMERSON

The success of teachers and healers and leaders lies in their being able and willing to bear witness to the Christ ideas active in the consciousness of those whom the Father draws to them, and not in their telling what they personally can do or have done.

MYRTLE FILLMORE

Let no man say there is no God
When all creation sings His praise.
The flaming bush,
The burgeoning tree,
The birds that carol joyfully
Proclaim His beauty and accord.

MARY G. HALE

Right thinking is everything, and if the children are taught to think rightly, we need have no fear for the future peace of the world.   LADY ASTOR

Naught but good can come to me,
This is Love's supreme decree.
Since I bar my door to hate,
What have I to fear, O Fate?
                    ELLA WHEELER WILCOX

We do not need more material development; we need more spiritual development. We do not need more intellectual power; we need more moral power. We do not need more knowledge; we need more character. We do not need more government; we need more culture. We do not need more law; we need more religion. We do not need more of the things that are seen; we need more of the things that are unseen.

                    CALVIN COOLIDGE

We can do anything, be anything, achieve any worthwhile goal we desire simply by the daily process of following Paul's admonition, "Have this mind in you, which was also in Christ Jesus."

                    RALPH RHEA

The most beautiful thing we can experience is the mysterious. It is the source of all true art and science. He to whom this emotion is a stranger, who can no longer pause to wonder and stand rapt in awe, is as good as dead; his eyes are closed. This insight into the mystery of life, coupled though it be with fear, has given rise to religion. To know that what is impenetrable really exists, manifesting itself as the highest wisdom and the most radiant beauty which our dull senses can comprehend—in their most primitive forms—this knowledge, this feeling, is at the center of true religiousness.

ALBERT EINSTEIN

I love to think of nature as an unlimited broadcasting station through which God speaks to us every day, every moment of our lives, if we will only tune in.

GEORGE WASHINGTON CARVER

He healed them all, all those who sought
    the Christ;
  He never questioned color, creed, or
    race.
His great compassion looked for but one
    sign:
  The light of faith upon a lifted face.

EUGENIA FINN

The wonderful principles that Jesus used in performing His so-called miracles are working here and now for all those who have faith in God as the source of their blessings and who are making the teachings of the Master practical in their daily thinking and living. "God is no respecter of persons."

MYRTLE FILLMORE

Above all, seek within, and bow at no human shrine. You have the same fountain of truth from which to draw as has the most favored individual on this planet, and you will never get unadulterated truth, until you evoke it within your own soul. This is the road all must eventually travel.

CHARLES FILLMORE

Go put your creed into your deed.

RALPH WALDO EMERSON

Hope ever urges on, and tells us tomorrow will be better.

OVID

One resolution I have made and always try to keep is this: To rise above little things.

JOHN BURROUGHS

Sue

Earth's crammed with heaven,
And every common bush afire with God.
ELIZABETH BARRETT BROWNING

Man's discovery of God is the most
wonderful story ever told, and whether he
admits it to himself or not, his need for
God is ever present.
CECIL B. DeMILLE

Anyone who expects to do good must not
expect people to roll stones out of his way
but must accept his lot calmly even if they
roll a few more into it.
ALBERT SCHWEITZER

There is a destiny which makes us
brothers, —
None goes his way alone:
All that we send into the lives of others
Comes back into our own.
EDWIN MARKHAM

Thinking is the talking of the soul with
itself.
PLATO

A poor workman blames his tools.
IMELDA O. SHANKLIN

A good impulse is born of love for man;
A part of God's divinely perfect plan.
Have you an urge to help Him? Well, you
    can!
  Act upon it!
                    HAZEL THOMAS WRIGHT

Listen to the exhortation of the dawn!
  Look to this day!
For it is life, the very life of life.
In its brief course lie all the
Verities and realities of your existence;
    The bliss of growth,
    The glory of action,
    The splendor of beauty;
For yesterday is but a dream,
And tomorrow is only a vision;
    But today, well lived, makes
Every yesterday a dream of happiness,
And every tomorrow a vision of hope.
Look well therefore to this day!
                A PASSAGE FROM THE SANSKRIT

Religion, not in the conventional but in
the broadest sense, helps me to have a
glimpse of the divine essence. This
glimpse is impossible without full
development of the moral sense. Hence
religion and morality are, for me,
synonymous terms. . . .
                    GANDHI

To every man there openeth
A way, and ways, and a way,
And the high soul climbs the high way,
And the low soul gropes the low;
And in between, on the misty flats,
The rest drift to and fro.
But to every man there openeth
A high way, and a low,
And every man decideth
The way his soul shall go.

JOHN OXENHAM

Persistently hold in view the wish to know the truth, and it will gradually be made manifest to you. Seek and you will find. It is the law that desire must precede fulfillment.

GRENVILLE KLEISER

Suppose an electric light bulb could say to the electricity, "You belong to me," and it could try to hold the electricity to itself instead of letting it shine out in light — what would happen? The bulb would break. So we in our human thinking break down under personal responsibility, trying to do God's work of shining instead of just letting His love shine out and His life flow out in blessing, or trying to hold to us that which is free Spirit.

MYRTLE FILLMORE

If we work upon marble, it will perish. If we work upon brass, time will efface it. If we rear temples, they will crumble to dust. But if we work upon men's immortal minds, if we imbue them with high principles, with the just fear of God and love of their fellow men, we engrave on those tablets something which no time can efface, and which will brighten and brighten to all eternity.

DANIEL WEBSTER

Wherever there's a shadow there's a light.

EDGAR LINTON

It is better to light one small candle than to curse the darkness.

CONFUCIUS

Prayer is the greatest force that we can wield. It is the greatest talent which God has given us. There is a democracy in this matter. We may differ among ourselves as to wealth, as to our social position, as to our educational equipment, as to native ability, as to our inherited characteristics; but in this matter of exercising the greatest force that is at work in the world today, we are on the same footing.

JOHN R. MOTT

If you are unsuccessful, if you are unhappy, look within yourself for the cause. God's storehouse is open to all. We can take from it what we will, but we should learn to use wisely the riches that we find there.

JANE PALMER

Nations are always conquered from the inside. So long as we are morally strong we shall be strong in every other way. Our only dangerous foes are within the country, not without. Those who perpetrate injustice, those who appeal to violence, those who stir up class hatred are the men whom we as a nation have to dread and against whom we have to protect ourselves. Liberty and independence, law and order, are not preserved by written constitutions and statutes; not by police and armies; not by wealth and success, but by the morality of the people. The government and institutions of a country cannot rise much higher than the general ethical level. We cannot expect a government to be honest while the people are dishonest.

EDWIN E. SLOSSON

Practice the presence of God just as you would practice music.

H. EMILIE CADY

Every word of Truth you think or speak is a power for good. It works immediately to create new conditions of harmony, righteousness, health, and peace.

CLARA PALMER

All service ranks the same with God, There is no last nor first.

ROBERT BROWNING

That which you are today is the fulfillment of yesterday's aspiration; that which you are tomorrow will be the achievement of today's vision.

FAYETTE M. DRAKE

The higher the ideal of yourself, the more rapid your spiritual growth; see yourself ideally as divine, and you will become it.

ARCHDEACON WILBERFORCE

May God's wisdom guide you.

May His power protect you, His bounty supply you, His love surround you as the waters surround the fishes of the sea;

And may the clear consciousness of His healing presence abide with you each hour of every day.

EVA EVANS ANDERSON

We hear men often speak of seeing God in the stars and the flowers; but they will never be truly religious till they learn to know Him in each other also, where He is most easily, yet most rarely, discovered.

J. R. LOWELL

Thou couldst not have sought me if thou hadst not already found me.

PASCAL

Are you in earnest? Seize this very
          minute;
What you can do, or dream you can, begin
          it;
Boldness has genius, power and magic in
          it.
Only engage, and then the mind grows
          heated,
Begin, and the work is half completed.

JOHANN WOLFGANG VON GOETHE

Light is the shadow of God.

PLATO

The wise and good man harvests the good not by what he does or by what happens to him, but by what he is.

PLOTINUS

Therefore, come what may, hold fast to
love. Though men should rend your heart,
let them not embitter or harden it. We win
by tenderness; we conquer by forgiveness.

W. ROBERTSON

For all thy wondrous works, O Lord,
　I lift my song of praise;
For blessings more than tongue can tell,
　For joyous work-filled days.
I thank Thee, Lord, for home and friends,
　For faith in what is good,
For love that taught me how to give
　All that I can, and should.
The meager crumbs that I have shared
　With others in Thy name
Returned to me a hundredfold
　As all my blessings came
Straight from the bounty of Thy love,
　A source that ceases never
And fills my overflowing cup
　With peace and joy forever.

MABEL CLARE THOMAS

It is your mission to express all that you
can imagine God to be. Let this be your
standard of achievement; never lower it,
nor allow yourself to be belittled by the
cry of sacrilege. You can attain to everything that you can imagine.

CHARLES FILLMORE

In all things throughout the world the man who looks for the crooked will see the crooked; and the man who looks for the straight will see the straight.

JOHN RUSKIN

I went to church last Sunday
  In a cathedral vast and high;
The paneled walls were pine trees.
  And the dome the bright blue sky.
I knelt on the pine-strewn carpet
  Of moss and tender sod;
My spirit went singing, winging
  Very near to God!

ELIZABETH GUION HESS

Religion is not a method; it is a life, a communion with God, a calm and deep enthusiasm, a love which radiates, a force which acts, a happiness which overflows.

H. F. AMIEL

Jesus Christ made it clear that God expresses His love in cleansing and healing. We must make room for Christ until His perfect love takes up all the room. Then we shall be conscious of and experience His guidance and sustaining power increasingly.

JOHN MAILLARD

To be meek, yet bold; enthusiastic, but not impulsive; patient, but not complacent; long-suffering, but not resigned; frank, yet tactful; humble, yet with self-respect; repentant, but never dispirited; happy over our achievements, but never satisfied with them; old in experience, yet young in spirit; jealous of our own creeds, while respecting the religious beliefs of others.

ANDREW HAMMER

I am owner of the sphere,
Of the seven stars and the solar year,
Of Caesar's hand and Plato's brain,
Of Lord Christ's heart and Shake-
     spear's strain.

RALPH WALDO EMERSON

If any one could tell you the shortest, surest way to all happiness and all perfection, he must tell you to make it a rule to yourself to thank and praise God for everything that happens to you. For it is certain that whatever seeming calamity happens to you, if you thank and praise God for it, you turn it into a blessing. Could you therefore work miracles, you could not do more for yourself than by this thankful spirit; for it . . . turns all that it touches into happiness.

WILLIAM LAW

The kindly word that falls today may bear
its fruit tomorrow.

GANDHI

When Truth has had its whole effect on
our minds, it will gain its fullness of
authority by becoming to us simply the
echo of our own thought. We shall find
that we think as Christ thought. Thus we
shall be one with Him, and with Him one
with the Father.

RALPH WALDO EMERSON

Paradise is always where love dwells.

JEAN PAUL RICHTER

"Be still, and know!" the Scripture says.
So I shall heed through all my days
The still small voice of God whose word,
Through my inner calmness heard,
Shows me hourly where to go;
And as His words of wisdom flow
Through heart and soul I clearly see
The course His love reveals to me!

PAULINE HAVARD

You can have neither a greater nor a lesser
dominion than that over yourself.

LEONARDO DA VINCI

I saw a crystal of the snow
Repose beneath a lens, and lo,
Perfection was in every line
Of its most intricate design.

I asked, "Why do you have unmarred
This wondrous beauty, silver-starred,
This loveliness without a flaw?"
It gently said, "I kept the law."

I saw where June's soft zephyr blows
The smiling beauty of a rose;
Each petal of its blushing face
Was rare in color and in grace.

I asked, "How came you to possess
So rare a wealth of loveliness?"
I waited for some voice of awe;
It simply said, "I kept the law."

CLARENCE E. FLYNN

Some men have thousands of reasons why
they cannot do what they want to, when all
they need is one reason why they can.

WILLIS R. WHITNEY

Love is the greatest thing that God can
give us; for He himself is love; and it is the
greatest thing we can give to God; for it
will also give ourselves and carry with it
all that is ours.

JEREMY TAYLOR

A person who impoverishes his body with the idea that it is only the spirit that counts, displays as warped a view of truth as the man who starves and neglects the spirit and cares only for the body. In God's plan the development should progress in harmonious order, with equally divided attention. The spirit requires a noble instrument in order to carry out the full will of God.

HENRY B. WILSON

Truth is within ourselves; it takes no rise
From outward things, whate'er you may
    believe.
There is an inmost center in us all, where
    truth
abides in fullness. . . .
and, to Know, Rather consists in opening
    out a way
Whence the imprisoned splendor may
    escape,
Than in effecting entry for a light
Supposed to be without.

ROBERT BROWNING

Serene, I fold my hands and wait,
  Nor care for wind, or tide, or sea;
I rave no more 'gainst Time or Fate,
  For, lo! my own shall come to me.

JOHN BURROUGHS

In your hands will be placed the exact results of your thoughts; you will receive that which you earn, no more, no less. Whatever your present environment may be, you will fall, remain, or rise with your thoughts, your wisdom, desire, as great as your dominant aspiration.

JAMES ALLEN

Prosperity is the result of complying with definite laws that are revealed by the Spirit of truth within. Those who are prosperous and successful are the people who have a rich consciousness . . . the ones who have developed their innate abilities and used the success-producing ideas that have come to them.

MYRTLE FILLMORE

No virtue is higher than love to all men, and there is no loftier aim in life than to do good to all men.

CONFUCIUS

The best help is not to bear the troubles of others for them, but to inspire them with courage and energy to bear their burdens for themselves and meet the difficulties of life bravely.

LUBBOCK

Let every dawn of morning be to you as the beginning of life, and every setting sun be to you as its close; then let every one of those short lives leave its sure record of some kindly thing done for others, some goodly strength or knowledge gained for yourself.

JOHN RUSKIN

As you think, you travel; and as you love, you attract. You are today where your thoughts have brought you; you will be tomorrow where your thoughts take you. You cannot escape the result of your thoughts, but you can endure and learn, can accept and be glad.

JAMES ALLEN

Let us labor for an Inward Stillness,
An inward stillness, and an Inward Heal-
    ing;
That perfect Silence, where the lips and
    heart
Are still, and we no longer entertain
Our own imperfect thoughts and vain
    opinions;
But God alone speaks in us, and we wait
In singleness of Heart, that we may know
His Will, and in the Silence of our spirits,
That we may do That only.

HENRY W. LONGFELLOW

I believe that the reason of life is for each of us simply to grow in love.

I believe that this growth in love will contribute more than any other force to establish the kingdom of God on earth . . . to replace a social life in which division, falsehood, and violence are all-powerful, with a new order in which humanity, truth, and brotherhood will reign.

TOLSTOY

Mind is the Master-power that moulds and
     makes,
And Man is Mind, and evermore he takes
The Tool of Thought, and, shaping what he
     wills,
Brings forth a thousand joys, a thousand
     ills: —
He thinks in secret, and it comes to pass,
Environment is but his looking-glass.

JAMES ALLEN

I know this world is ruled by infinite intelligence. It required infinite intelligence to create it, and it requires infinite intelligence to keep it on its course. Everything that surrounds us — everything that exists — proves that there are infinite laws behind it. There can be no denying this fact. It is mathematical in its precision.

THOMAS ALVA EDISON

Listen to your inner voice; cultivate the good, the pure, the God within you. The divine spark is within you. Fan it into flame by right thinking, right living, and right doing.

CHARLES FILLMORE

If a man is imbued with a generous mind, this is the best kind of nobility.

PLATO

Endeavor to be always patient of the faults and imperfections of others; for thou hast many faults and imperfections of thine own that require forbearance.

THOMAS à KEMPIS

Health enough to make work a pleasure. Wealth enough to support your needs. Strength to battle with difficulties and overcome them. Grace enough to confess your sins and forsake them. Patience enough to toil until some good is accomplished. Charity enough to see some good in your neighbor. Love enough to move you to be useful and helpful to others. Faith enough to make real the things of God. Hope enough to remove all anxious fears of the future.

JOHANN WOLFGANG VON GOETHE

Self-trust is the first secret of success, the belief that if you are here the authorities of the universe put you here, and for cause, or with some task strictly appointed you in your constitution, and so long as you work at that you are well and successful.

RALPH WALDO EMERSON

If thou art not able to make thyself that which thou wishest, how canst thou expect to mold another in conformity to thy will?

THOMAS à KEMPIS

Above all, no reproaches about what is past and cannot be altered! How can a man live at all if he did not grant absolution every night to himself and all his fellows!

JOHANN WOLFGANG VON GOETHE

The actions of men are the best interpreters of their thoughts.

JOHN LOCKE

There are many people who fear solitude, confusing it no doubt with loneliness. But in solitude, as nowhere else, there always is, or there may be, divine companionship.

ARCHIBALD RUTLEDGE

Hail! Ye small, sweet courtesies of life, for
smooth do ye make the road of it.
LAURENCE STERNE

Circumstances will only deteriorate if you
allow anger and emotion to carry you away
when things go wrong. You should quietly
direct your thoughts to God who dwells
within.
MASAHARU TANIGUCHI

A Sundial in our garden
    Marks just the brightest hours,
And does not tell the time when
    A storm beat down the flowers.

Then why should I be holding
    This burden overlong?
Dark times are times for molding
    A still more lovely song.

Since darkness is but absence
    Of consciousness of light,
Quite quickly in light's presence
    It disappears from sight.

So why should I be pining
    And marking hours of gloom?
The light is always shining
    Within my inner room!
KATHERINE J. H. CLINGERMAN

46

There is no place where God is not—no place where His love, His kindness, His generosity, His righteousness do not prevail.

SILENT UNITY

In all the universe there is no greater power than the power of God's love, no greater security than the security of His love, no greater riches, no greater freedom, peace, or happiness than that which is yours this moment in the love that enfolds you, even the love of the Infinite.

CLARA PALMER

Your way lies plain before your face; if you have courage walk in it.

JOHN WESLEY

It is a good, safe rule to sojourn in every place as if you meant to spend your life there, never omitting an opportunity of doing a kindness, speaking a true word, or making a friend.

JOHN RUSKIN

He who wishes to revenge injuries by reciprocal hatred will live in misery.

SPINOZA

47

Be noble! And the nobleness that lies in other men, sleeping but never dead, will rise in majesty to meet thine own.

JAMES RUSSELL LOWELL

There's the wise thrush,
He sings each song twice over,
Lest you should think he never could
    recapture
That first fine, careless rapture.

ROBERT BROWNING

The only conceivable way of bringing about a reconstruction of our world on new lines is first of all to become new men ourselves under the old circumstances, and then as a society in a new frame of mind so to smooth out the opposition between nations that a condition of true civilization may again become possible. Everything else is more or less wasted labor, because we are thereby building not on the spirit, but on what is merely external.

ALBERT SCHWEITZER

Man is ever in the presence of an infinite and eternal energy from which all things proceed.

HERBERT SPENCER

Enthusiasm is the greatest asset in the world. It overwhelms and engulfs all obstacles. It is nothing more nor less than faith in action.

HENRY CHESTER

He that does good to another does good also to himself, not only in the consequence but in the very act. For the consciousness of well-doing is in itself ample reward.   SENECA

Christ has no body now on earth but yours, no hands but yours, no feet but yours; yours are the eyes through which is to look out Christ's compassion on the world, yours are the feet with which He is to go about doing good, and yours are the hands with which He is to bless us now.

ST. TERESA

Do something for somebody, somewhere
  While jogging along life's road;
Help someone to carry his burden,
  And lighter will grow your load.
Do something for somebody always,
  Whatever may be your creed—
There's nothing on earth can help you
  So much as a kindly deed.

ANONYMOUS

THE GOLDEN RULE
OF RELIGIONS

Do as you would be done by.

PERSIAN

Do not that to a neighbor which you would take ill from him.

GRECIAN

What you would not wish done to yourself, do not unto others.

CHINESE

One should seek for others the happiness one desires for oneself.

BUDDHIST

He sought for others the good he desired for himself. Let him pass on.

EGYPTIAN

All things whatsoever ye would that men should do to you, do ye even so to them.

CHRISTIAN

Let none of you treat his brother in a way he himself would dislike to be treated.

MOHAMMEDAN

The true rule in life is to guard and do by the things of others as they do by their own.

HINDU

The law imprinted on the hearts of all men is to love the members of society as themselves.   ROMAN

Whatsoever you do not wish your neighbor to do to you, do not unto him. This is the whole law. The rest is a mere exposition of it.   JEWISH

I invoiced all my goods today:
    It's hard to comprehend
How much one has to give away
    To relative and friend.

I gave my sister extra smiles
    And a special, kindly word.
I told her that her laughter was
    The sweetest I had heard.

I gave our gardener time to tell
    Of flowers in other lands.
I made him glad by telling him
    How tender are his hands.

And yet since giving here and there
    The things I did today,
Tomorrow I shall have just twice
    As much to give away.
                ENOLA CHAMBERLIN

Kind words are the music of the world. They have a power which seems to be beyond natural causes, as if they were some angel's song which had lost its way and come to earth.

F. W. FABER

Our doubts are traitors,
And make us lose the good we oft might
　　win
　By fearing to attempt.

WILLIAM SHAKESPEARE

The beauty of the world and the orderly arrangement of everything celestial makes us confess that there is an excellent and eternal nature, which ought to be worshiped and admired by all mankind.

CICERO

Speak to him, thou, for he hears,
and spirit with Spirit can meet
Closer is he than breathing
and nearer than hands and feet.

TENNYSON

Those who bring sunshine to the lives of others cannot keep it from themselves.

J. M. BARRIE

There is nothing noble in being superior to some other man. The true nobility is in being superior to your previous self.

HINDU SAYING

Laurel crowns cleave to deserts,
And power to him who power exerts.
Hast not thy share? On winged feet
Lo! it flyeth thee to meet.
All that nature made thine own,
Floating in air or pent in stone,
Will rive the hills, and swim the sea,
And like thy shadow follow thee.

RALPH WALDO EMERSON

If there is righteousness in the heart, there will be beauty in the character. If there is beauty in the character, there will be harmony in the home. If there is harmony in the home, there will be order in the nation. When there is order in the nation, there will be peace in the world.

CHINESE PROVERB

Truth is. It is changeless, eternal, and it is undisturbed by enemies. It is mighty and prevails—not by struggle, but just by being. He who opposes it has a one-sided fight.

EDNA L. CARTER

Branches are bare against gray skies;
  Dry leaves are carpeting the ground.
Wild geese have long since gone their way.
  Bleak autumn breezes sound

Their warning: Winter time is near,
  And many a storm with icy blast
Of wind will sing a sunless song
  As it goes rushing past.

Gardens are sleeping, soon to be
  Hidden beneath long drifts of snow;
Yet fallen leaf and barren branch
  And sleeping gardens know

That nothing ends. As seasons come
  And go beneath eternal skies,
Life's patterns move, to merge or change,
  But nothing ever dies.
                    ROWENA CHENEY

Two men looked out through their prison
bars;
  The one saw mud, and the other, stars.
        ROBERT LOUIS STEVENSON

The more we see of beauty everywhere — in
nature, in life, in man and child, in work
and rest, in the outward and inward
world — the more we see of God.
          JAMES FREEMAN CLARKE

When faith is genuine, circumstances that appear to be evil are compelled to get into line with God's good plan.

LOWELL FILLMORE

The knowledge and ability you crave for your chosen work resides within yourself. As co-creator in the universal plan, you are entrusted with some part in the great design, and can summon at will the wisdom and power needed for the purpose assigned you.

ELIZA A. GOLDIE

The fact is that the people of the present age are more open to spiritual inspiration than the people of any preceeding age. The race has been educated to a point where a very large number are ready to receive, with open mind, the thoughts of Deity. We are undoubtedly in the beginning of that time predicted by the prophets of old, when every man would know the Lord from the greatest even unto the least.

CHARLES FILLMORE

Out of the lowest depth there is a path to the loftiest height.

RALPH WALDO EMERSON

My baby goes to school today—
With eager steps he leaves my side.
I smile, and wave good-by, and pray
(Blinking my foolish tears away)
That You, dear Lord, will guide

Not only my small son, but me.
Teach me, O Lord, that I may know
How to release him—set him free
To seek You first, that he may be
Secure, wherever he may go.

And let no longing to possess
Or bind too fast with family ties
Distort my vision, make me less
A mother. Heavenly Father, bless
My little boy; and make me wise,

That I may help this little one
To put his loving faith in You.
And may his learning, here begun,
Result in happy work well done,
With You to guide him all life through.
                    ROWENA CHENEY

"According to your faith be it done unto
you." All of us must hitch our faith to the
divine ideas that make for abundance of
manifest good. Then we have a foundation
upon which to build our castle of health,
happiness, and prosperity.
                    MYRTLE FILLMORE

Every man is king in his own mental domain, and his subjects are his thoughts. . . . The body is the instrument of the mind, and the mind looks to the spirit for its inspiration.

CHARLES FILLMORE

Let not thy mind run on what thou lackest as much as on what thou hast already.

MARCUS AURELIUS ANTONINUS

True happiness consists not in the knowledge of good things, but in good life; not in understanding, but in living understandingly. Neither is it great learning, but good will that joins men to God.

CORNELIUS AGRIPPA

The goal is already stated. My consolation and my happiness are to be found in service of all that lives, because the divine essence is the sum total of all life.

GANDHI

The only heresy
Is not to love another,
For we are fashioned to be
Keepers of our brother.

HAROLD WHALEY

Friendship is the bloom of the love of God in the soul of man.

RICHARD LYNCH

Faith enough to move mountains comes of using faith enough to move grains of sand.

GARDNER HUNTING

If we are tormented with grief or anxiety, the sure remedy is to look within and find God in the secret chamber of our own soul. For there God dwells, and the invitation is that we commune with Him.

HENRY THOMAS HAMBLIN

Turn your problem over to God and forget it. But do not forget God.

LOWELL FILLMORE

Let us impart all the blessings we possess, or ask for ourselves, to the whole family of mankind.

GEORGE WASHINGTON

Don't say things. What you are stands over you the while and thunders so that I cannot hear what you say to the contrary.

RALPH WALDO EMERSON

True faith is victorious over every adverse condition, overcoming every human weakness, supplying every human need; it will not stoop to strive with earthly adverse circumstances; it simply rises above them and they become subject to its will.

LOWELL FILLMORE

A tree that it takes both arms to encircle grew from a tiny rootlet. A many-storied pagoda is built by placing one brick upon another brick. A journey of three thousand miles is begun by a single step.

LAO-TSE

The steps of faith fall on the seeming void, but find the rock beneath.

WHITTIER

Before we can bring happiness to others, we first must be happy ourselves; nor will happiness abide within us unless we confer it on others.

MAURICE MAETERLINCK

Truths are what pray in man, and a man is continually at prayer when he lives according to truths.

SWENDENBORG

I sought Thee at a distance, and did not know that Thou wast near. I sought Thee abroad, and behold, Thou wast within me.
ST. AUGUSTINE

Devote to better living the energy that you could spend in criticism.
IMELDA O. SHANKLIN

What a new face courage puts on everything! A determined man, by his very attitude and the tone of his voice, puts a stop to defeat and begins to conquer.
RALPH WALDO EMERSON

God is the fact of the fact, the life of the life, the soul of the soul, the incomprehensible, the sum of all contradictions, the unit of all diversity; he who knows Him, knows Him not; he who is without Him, is full of Him; turn your back upon Him, then turn your back upon gravity, upon air, upon light. He is not a being, yet apart from Him there is no being—there is no apart from Him.
JOHN BURROUGHS

Great minds have purposes, others have wishes. WASHINGTON IRVING

Life for me is real, as I believe it to be a spark of the divine.

GANDHI

When anyone has offended me, I try to raise my soul so high that the offense cannot reach it. SOCRATES

Field and forest, vale and mountain,
  Flowery meadow, flashing sea,
Chanting bird and flowing fountain,
  Call us to rejoice in Thee.

HENRY VAN DYKE

Faith strengthens us, enlightens us, for all endeavors and endurances; with faith we can do all, and dare all, and life itself has a thousand times been joyfully given away.

CARLYLE

If we expect to receive anything from God, who "giveth to all men liberally, and upbraideth not," we must turn our faces toward Him like little children, and open our entire being to his incoming. We must not shut Him out by either a tense, rigid, mental condition of anxiety, or by an unforgiving spirit.

H. EMILIE CADY

"The leeks and the cucumbers
of Egypt," they lamented—
as they trekked reluctantly
toward the promised land
and freedom.
Later, by the waters of Babylon
they wept, remembering Zion.
The moral: not so much lack
of gratitude for their heritage,
but unseeing eyes that should have seen
holy ground wherever they walked.
It is not here nor there
nor in between, but in all places
and in all times
that God acts for our good.
From each experience, in hearts
that receive receptively,
a facet is burnished, completing,
step by step, the perfect gem
that was, is, and always shall be
our life in Him.

HAROLD WHALEY

Finally, brethren, whatsoever things are
true, whatsoever things are honest, whatsoever things are just, whatsoever things
are pure, whatsoever things are lovely,
whatsoever things are of good report; if
there be any virtue, and if there be any
praise, think on these things.

PHILIPPIANS 4:8

UNITY SCHOOL OF CHRISTIANITY
Unity Village, Missouri 64065

Printed in the United States of America   146F-4058-15M-4-80